The Foundation for Purpose

Is

I0080189

Relationship

McDougal & Associates
Servants of Christ and Stewards of the
Mysteries of God

The Foundation for Purpose

Is

Relationship

by

Apostle Reginald Wilson

Published by:

McDougal & Associates
18896 Greenwell Springs Road
Greenwell Springs, LA 70739
www.thepublishedword.com

McDougal & Associates is dedicated to the spreading of the
Gospel of Jesus Christ to as many people as possible
in the shortest time possible.

ISBN 978-1-940461-38-0

Printed in the US, the UK and Australia
For Worldwide Distribution

What Others Are Saying

"The people of the world seem to understand that knowing the right person could be just what they need for their 'big break,' but the missing link is God. It is not coincidence or happenstance when someone comes along who propels us to our future. *The Foundation for Purpose Is Relationship* is not just another nice concept. It is essential and critical for God's purpose to be established in your life."

Regina Wilson Davis
Chemical Engineer

"Apostle Reggie Wilson is a man totally sold out to the Kingdom principle of servant leadership empowered through foundational relationships that can transform the Church and the nation, when embraced by godly men and women positioned to fulfill His purposes for their lives. When self-promotion can be relegated to irrelevance, and relationship can genuinely be installed as, not only foundational, but as truly indispensable, then great leaders will not only rise up; they will be raised up."

Peter Felsch
Australia

"I am so grateful for this great work being penned, to heal so many of God's people at a time when many are going back to the world looking for healing, when God's medicine of humility is what we really need."

Pastor Dawn Harmon
Lancaster, Pennsylvania

Dedication

In memory of my father, **Edward Wilson Sr.,** who passed away on September 19, 1987.

In memory of my mother-in-law, **Luvenia Johnson**, deceased April 28, 2012.

In appreciation of my mother, **Elise V. Batiste**. As of this writing, she is 86 and still going strong.

In honor of my wife, **Dr. Vera Mae Jackson Wilson,** who remains by my side.

I am thankful to God for these four pillars who played a role in my discovering meaningful relationships.

Special Tribute

To **Dionee Powe Williams** (March 26, 1963 — June 23, 2011), my first publisher. She played such a unique role in making this book possible. After a ferocious bout with cancer, she went on to her eternal reward. Our loss was Heaven's gain.

To her widow, Keith Williams, and her mother Gracie and her family: Dionee completed her assignment. As you keep your heads to the sky, may you know the unlimited love of the Creator and realize that He is making known her heart through the many she inspired to do what only God in them could do, making their dreams become reality. Her vision was so big that it could only be fulfilled after she had left her earthly tabernacle. Her legacy will live on.

Acknowledgements

Where should I start? There are so many people who have contributed to my life over the years, and all of them helped the message of this book to evolve. I must thank a few of them:

I wish to thank all of my friends who prayed and walked with me and had the courage to hang in there throughout the years. I have learned valuable lessons from you that have blessed me and benefited me in the areas of character, integrity and destiny. Thank you for your loyal friendship.

Special thanks to those men and women of God who have labored in the cities and nations that I have visited. I appreciate your willingness to take a risk with me, by inviting me to speak or by being my friend. Your example gave me wisdom, and your servanthood taught me hospitality. Having this kind of fellowship has allowed me to use our relationships as the testing ground for my future. Our conflicts have helped to develop my humility. Your hope, love and patience have taught me what this book is really about.

Again I must credit Dionee Powe Williams for the many hours of editing, arranging and laying out this material. She worked with me even when things got tough. The original project would not have been completed in such a timely manner and with excellence had it not been for her and the patience of her husband Keith, which allowed her to burn the midnight oil to accomplish it. I am grateful.

There were many others who came along at crucial times to support me when their services were needed.

Many thanks, to my Muslim friend, Samimah of St. Louis, Missouri, and Angela Wimberly of Bloomfield, Connecticut, who both believed in this book and encouraged me to get it done.

Thank you, Danielle Ojeabulu, for editing.

Thanks to Tracey Cooper, Regina Wilson Davis and Danielle Clay for your editorial contribution. Your spirit to serve gave me strength.

Thanks to Kimberly Williamson for the second editing and to Kim V. Davis, my book and marketing consultant, for your professional service in handling multitasking.

I must also acknowledge two more editors who stepped up to the plate to improve this release: Angela Aubry, a local editor, and John Petersen of Zambia. All of these made it a better book, and I love and appreciate you.

Finally, there are not enough words in the English language to express my appreciation to my wife and family. You were my joy, motivation and support to finish strong. My girls — Danielle, Regina and Tomoro — and my son Reginald Jr., have graciously allowed me to experience years of global travel as I developed new relationships. I have been away from the home countless days, yet their unconditional love remains beyond that which any father could ask for or imagine. Thank you for your sacrifice.

To the most important person in my life, my friend and loving wife Vera: you have faithfully stood by my side since we met in New Orleans more than nearly forty years ago. Your firm, sweet way of speaking the truth in love has made me become the best man, father, husband and writer I could be. Heaven knew I would need a suitable helpmate to someday assist me to grow into maturity. Thank you, my "Honey Bun," my dearest Sweetheart, Vee-Mae, for allowing me to finally complete this book and for sticking until the end. I must say this again: without you, neither this book, nor the mass amount of relationships I have developed through the years would be possible. You are special, just for providing a warm home as a haven for my rest after projects like this one are done. You are the greatest, my angel sent from God. I'm eternally grateful to Him for putting us together forever.

Being confident of this very thing, that he which hath begun a good work in you will perform it until the day of Jesus Christ.

Philippians 1:6

Contents

Foreword

One of the primary benefits of travel, especially outside of the continental limits of the United States, is adventure. Such adventures can be both memorable and stimulating. I have had the pleasure of travelling abroad with Apostle Reggie Wilson on a number of occasions during the more than thirty years we have been friends, and I can say without question that there have been few dull moments while travelling with him.

More than once during our journeys we have found ourselves on some back road outside of a city in an old vehicle that had broken down. Because both of us were mechanically challenged, we had to rely on other resources. On several of these adventures, I considered myself very blessed to be with someone who is relationally adept. No matter where we were, Apostle Reggie always seemed to find some stranger who, in a very short time, treated us as if we were lifelong friends. It seemed as though they had been planted there for just that occasion. I'm not ignorant of the fact that it was God, but Apostle Reggie was the instrument, and his God-given gift of making friends quickly was the means.

In this book, *The Foundation for Purpose Is Relationship*, Apostle Reggie shares with you valuable principles that have been marinated in personal experiences throughout his entire life. I have already read the book several times and have gleaned something new each time. It is practical, and yet it is profound.

The lessons Brother Reggie has learned (and, I dare say, is still learning) have not always come easily. I know this from personal experience because I have been there when he walked through some of them.

Finally, may I say that this book will both challenge and motivate you to anticipate new relationships and carefully nurture the existing ones. Bear in mind that all relationships are God's building blocks in His intended destiny for your life.

Leo De Jesus
Lion of Judah Unlimited Ministries
Gretna, Louisiana

Introduction

Years ago a gentleman shared a message that was destined to help me — and many others — break through our limitations and move to a place of significance. His sudden and unexpected conference appearance will never be forgotten because it served as a catalyst to transform his own life as well as many others, both here in America and in the world at large.

In those days, when someone was invited to speak at this particular conference, their rise to fame became inevitable. Today, this might be known as the "Oprah Touch " or the "Midas Touch " because it brought great success, wealth and relationships to those who had previously been unknown.

This annual conference, held in Tulsa, Oklahoma, brought a unique grace and opened doors for speakers such as Joyce Meyer, Michael Pitts, and T.D. Jakes (just to name a few). After speaking there, they experienced significant growth in their ministries that benefited God's Kingdom and the world.

At one of these conferences, I heard a profound message later reproduced in a video. It was entitled "Finding Your Purpose," and it changed my life. This Azusa Street Conference was the vision of the great Carlton Pearson, and that powerful message was brought forth by none other than the late Dr. Myles Munroe of Nassau, Bahamas.

More than twenty-five years ago now, I had the opportunity to meet him, and he agreed to spend some time with me, so that we could get to know each other better. We began exchanging ideas, while riding together in the car. As we were approaching my home in Marrero, in a very friendly manner, he said to me, "You don 't really know who you are sitting beside, do you?"

I smiled and, without hesitation or apology, immediately answered, "You don't really know who you are sitting beside!"

He laughed, and so did I. Then I said, "You see, the foundation for purpose is relationship, and the secret of God's power is timing!"

Dr. Munroe responded by saying, "That sounds like a book you need to write!"

"It will be. It will be!" I replied. It was not until twenty years later that I first presented the book. And now, here it is in its latest edition.

Why have I long insisted that *The Foundation for Purpose Is Relationship*? All of us humans were created to have a relationship of some sort with other people. Learning the skills necessary to form and maintain proper relationships can make all the difference in the value you give to others and the value they give back to you. That's what this book is all about.

Apostle Reggie Wilson
Marrero, Louisiana

CHAPTER 1

Dare to Believe in Your Destiny

Hope deferred maketh the heart sick: but when
the desire cometh, it is a tree of life.

Proverbs 13:12

I was conceived out of a relationship nearing its end and heading for divorce, where all too often pain and disappointment assail. Sentenced to life in a single-family household, I, along with two other siblings, did have a loving mother who was dedicated to nurturing us, but life was hard. Who would have ever believed that out of such challenging circumstances God had predestined and preordained a meaningful lifetime assignment and destiny for such a one as this, for such a one as me?

Along the way, no one ever told me that God would someday release me to many nations. In fact, I didn't have a clue about what might emerge in this process called *life*. I didn't realize that the process would come with good and bad experiences in relationships and that those good relationships would someday lead me to my God-assigned destiny.

> No one ever told me that God would someday release me to many nations!

My Wilderness

It was illness and later the snares of the drug scene that eventually led me to my wilderness of desperation, where I found myself thirsting and searching for a wellspring of life. There was a call deep inside that eventually forced me to discover that *The Foundation for Purpose Is Relationship.*

Our struggle in life is to learn how to navigate a path that will lead us to personal peace and our particular niche. There are so many wounded and hurting hearts who do not know how to find nor experience good relationships. In my desperation, I was given the opportunity to transform my sick heart into a tree of life. In the process, I discovered that life comes with many unpredictable challenges, and that is just the reality of things. In fact, there will be many tough encounters, and this will be true as long as we have breath in our bodies.

A Precise Destiny

It was amazing to imagine that there was a precise destiny carved out just for me. Finding that destiny required hope and a faith in a utopia, a solitary place where one's dreams could become a reality. Unfortunately, a lack of patience in the process and the immature mind-set of adolescence often cause us to place our expectations in people, rather than embracing and learning to maximize each season of life.

Somehow we must find release from living with constant feelings of blame, guilt or the sense that someone should have warned us about the perils of life. Or, perhaps even more so, that someone should have taken the responsibility to at least prepare us for the misfortunes that come in navigating a path to our destiny.

Fighting Disillusionment and Disappointment

Sooner or later, we all experience the disillusionment and disappointment of feeling that we have been given "the short end of the stick." Our "short stick" may represent a lack of training, a lack of information or a lack of the proper mentoring needed to fulfill the tasks assigned to our lives. The truth is that every assignment has a built-in process of life lessons specifically designed to prepare us for our destiny. We just haven't discovered them yet.

The key is to understand that nothing is an end in itself. Everything is connected to people, people with issues and problems in their lives. No one ever told me that I would someday fly from nation to nation as part of my destiny, because of the relationships I had developed.

Learning to Respond with the Right Attitude

I had to learn to respond with the right attitude, a positive perspective and greater hope. Every situation and individual was potentially part of a divine connection, and it was vitally important to understand that God gives everyone an opportunity to make a heart connection with others. These connections can open doors to our destiny and provide the foundation for healthy relationships.

My origin and humble beginnings had no power to determine my destiny, though such things certainly can impact our outlook, deferring our hope for a brighter day. Trusting in people, circumstances and self will diminish or defer hope because of their limited ability to impact our destiny. No individual has the power to ensure a desired outcome with any degree of certainty.

When hope is deferred, our dreams are put off until a future time. This is often the result of placing too much trust in circumstances, people and our own ability. God, in His infinite wisdom, has set our course in life. Only He has the correct answers to our struggle and strife. Hope is not given to be deferred, but rather to help us get from the now to the ultimate promise.

Hope Is an Action Word

Hope is an action word. It has the ability to strengthen and encourage our hearts to meet life's challenges. It speaks to our soul and says, "You don 't have to be down. You don 't have to be discouraged. And, no matter what, don't give up! Do not turn hope off!" This gift is provided to prevent us from throwing in the towel. Discouragement, deferred dreams and disappointments may have conspired to cause you to turn your internal hope switch off. If that is the case, your first step is to turn it on again and make it work for you. It's time to move forward.

The question is: once our hope has been turned off, how can it be turned back on again? I believe the answer lies in gaining an understanding of relationships. It is through our relationships that we will acquire the information and skills needed for life. Understanding relationships will help prepare and propel your way through many dilemmas.

Doing "Due Diligence"

The Word of God gives us the foundation, but we have to add due dili-gence. This "due diligence" consists of the works that must be added to our faith. As the Scriptures reveal, *"Faith without works is dead,"* (James 2:20). Just as in be-ginning a business, doing your due diligence bright-ens the path of your course, whatever it may be. Many people have great poten-tial and are sitting on ideas, dreams and visions that, if implemented, would not only change their lives, but also the lives of many oth-ers. Decide to perform your due diligence and see what God will do for you.

Hope has the ability to strengthen and encourage our hearts to meet life's challenges!

Through prophecies, promises and words of encouragement, hope can be revived Then, to keep a dream or vision alive, a healthy perspective on relationships is essential, for without it, you will remain trapped in lonely struggles.

Don't Remain Trapped in Disappointment

Disappointment only controls those who consider their temporary situation as the final word. This empowers and gives too much authority to our misfortunes with people and circumstances. Deferring hope can initiate and perpetuate a cycle of relationships and events that produce the same disappointing outcome. This will slow down our process, deplete our strength and break our momentum to move forward. In essence, it keeps us going nowhere.

The only cure to this problem is to make a purposeful decision to change. But change is not change until it is put into action. Prophetic and apostolic people are summoned by the Spirit to envision their future and contemplate great dreams. Thinking the good thoughts of purpose and destiny only prepare us for change. After meditating and seeing the possibilities, we can then walk into our change by faith. True change empowers us to take responsibility for our future.

Once we have begun the journey of hope, then we must make up our minds and hearts, through simple faith, to never again be a victim of another person's shortcomings. Instead, as we are working on change ourselves, we develop hope for others with similar issues, so that we can become a blessing to them.

Learning from Jesus

We can learn a valuable lesson by observing how Jesus walked in His relationship with His disciple Peter. He saw something in Peter's future that caused Him to believe that Peter would one day overcome his issues. Jesus, of course, as Master of relationships, was most skillful and, therefore, He is always the best example we could ever hope to follow. He said to Peter:

> *Simon, Simon, behold, Satan hath desired to have you, that he may sift you as wheat: but I have prayed for thee, that thy faith fail not: and when thou art converted, strengthen thy brethren.*   Luke 22:31-32

Jesus, as a man, never allowed His hope to be deferred because His expectations remained in God, the Father, our Creator. And He knew that just as God helped Him, He would also help Peter.

> All
> of
> our
> issues
> should
> be
> given
> to
> God
> to
> carry!

The Desire Will Come

We began this chapter with the first part of Proverbs 13:12. The rest of that verse says, "... *but when the desire cometh.*" It will come. The moral here is that we are to follow Jesus' example of patience as we wait for the manifestation of God's desire for our lives and the lives of others. We must not take control or become impatient. It is better to let go and surrender to the Father. Eventually, God's vision and plans (for us and others) will come to pass, and when they do, we and they will be as a tree of life.

A Matter of Our Free Will

How we relate to one another is really a matter of our free will. How we develop and maintain relationships is a matter of choice and time. No one else has to believe or receive you except God, and He is enough. By keeping it simple, the beginning and the end of hope continually rests in Him.

All of our issues should be given to God to carry. Relationship is the way to become and fulfill our destiny in God. He has a loving concern and perfect plan for each of us that makes up for what might be missing. Activate God's plan by seeking to understand those you walk with. Get to know them and don't try to make them change when they are not yet ready for change. Give it some time. Do *your* due diligence, and be prepared for the best and the worst in others.

Never be afraid of the possibility of betrayal; it's just a part of life. Simply refuse to empower the actions of others by not becoming a victim, paralyzed by what others do. Keep a positive attitude and respond graciously. Remember: mercy always triumphs over judgment.

A Great Testimony

In closing this chapter, allow me to share a great testimony of hope concerning my daughter Regina:

After graduating from high school at the top of her class, Regina was enrolled in college as an engineering student. We were very proud of her, as she continued to grow and move toward her expected end and hope for the future.

But then, just as Regina was entering her senior year in college, she came home one day and broke some shocking, hope-defying news to us. My precious daughter, a soon-to-be college graduate who had committed to keeping herself for her future husband, confessed to us that she was pregnant and did not know what to do.

Can you imagine what that was like for Regina, for my wife and for me? In a moment's time, our hope seemed to be on the way out the door. Pain, feelings of helplessness and weariness hit all of us at the same time, and our burden was great. All hope seemed to have suddenly dimmed.

Hope, however, is not meant to die. It can suddenly come to life at the most critical moments.

Believe me: hope is not meant to die, but to show itself alive in the worst of times. Through our relationship with God and with one another, Regina, my wife and myself somehow remained hopeful and began to visualize a greater victory ahead.

Hope Is Greater

Hope is greater than any feeling of shame or embarrassment. This crisis Regina experienced during her final undergraduate year would be used to build her character and prepare her for her future. We were so thankful that we'd had people who stood with us in those difficult times. Friends and other positive relationships, along with our trust in God, had encouraged us to stick together as a family and not give up on our destiny and purpose.

Today, our precious Regina has earned her MBA and works in the headquarters of a Fortune 500 petroleum company as an engineering executive. She is happily married and has blessed us with four of our twelve grandchildren. Her trial was one of our darkest seasons, but hope that seemed lost for a moment was turned back on, giving life to a brighter future. And just as it has happened for Regina and the rest of my family, it can happen for you and anyone else who will dare to believe in their destiny. Keep hope alive.

God's Word teaches us:

For he shall have judgment without mercy, that hath shewed no mercy; and mercy rejoiceth against judgment.   James 2:13

And hope maketh not ashamed; because the love of God is shed abroad in our hearts by the Holy Ghost which is given unto us.   Romans 5:5

Therefore hath he mercy on whom he will have mercy, and whom he will he hardeneth.
                                          Romans 9:18

Dare to believe in your destiny.

Discussion Questions for Chapter 1
"Dare To Believe In Your Destiny"

NAME: _____

DATE: _____

1. As you reflect upon your life, share one experience that has been used to give you a meaningful life assignment?

_____

_____

_____

_____

_____

2. Have you ever had your hope deferred? If so, how did it affect you?

_____

_____

_____

_____

_____

3. Based on the revelation shared on page 30, what is the only cure for a hope deferred?

_____

_____

_____

_____

_____

4. Why was hope given to us and what is the ability of hope in our lives? Explain.

_____

_____

_____

_____

_____

— Your Reflections —

Accidents and Sin Are a Certainty

Behold, I was shapen in iniquity; and in sin did my mother conceive me.　　　　Psalm 51:5

Thank God for insurance. Whether it is life, health, business or car insurance, everyone needs it and should have it. We live in a sinful and accident-prone world. Regardless of the perfection we desire to walk in, none of us is exempt from bad or evil things happening to us. Unfortunately, there are people around us who *think* they are exempt from such occurrences. They're not.

David's Understanding

King David had a deep understanding concerning the mystery of iniquity and cried these words in Psalm 51 to his God. It was his acknowledgement of his shortcomings and his need for divine help, and that is the foundation of a brokenness that pleases God.

Even as a king, David saw the need for sovereign protection and divine guidance. This kind of humility opened the door for honor to enter his life, providing him a greater capacity to serve other people with respect. An honest awareness of this type provides us a kind of peace and the acceptance to go forward in life without the fear of failure or the fear of being destroyed.

What God's Grace Gives Us

The honest truth is that God's grace gives us what we don't deserve — His unmerited favor. It is His mercy that detains what was due to transpire or materialize as a consequence of our iniquity and sins. So, no matter how self-righteous we are or how perfect we see ourselves, the rain falls on the just and the unjust (see Matthew 5:45). Keep in mind: one day you will need someone to forgive you. Mistakes happen, sin is real and accidents happen.

Just as accidents and sins are experienced by every individual and every family, the same is true in relationships. Even if you try to live righteously and without offense and do your best to avoid any accidents, let me assure you that they're going to happen anyway. To never expect rainy days is to be unprepared for problems and setbacks.

Even as a king, David saw the need for sovereign protection and divine guidance!

You might be in the right in a given situation, but because of the imperfections of others, harm can still come to you. Being right is not always the answer to every problem in life. However, having a right heart, with pure motives, can preserve your purpose, spare your relationships and heal your friendships. When it comes to an accident, you could be absolutely right, but you could also be dead. Such is life.

Missing the Mark

Having an accident means missing the mark, and you become a great marksman by practicing.

In the same way, you have to get out there and practice experiencing relationships in order to become skillful at it. Trial and error is necessary. I remember my mother's words: "You have to live and learn." You learn about people by being with people and not withdrawing from them. You must decide that nothing will cause you to remain on the sidelines and rob you of a fruitful and exciting life.

Something I learned from my wife about relationships is simple but profound. She would say, "You must dwell and walk with people according to your knowledge of them." If you know a person is a certain way, walk with them where they are. Don't insist on going somewhere they are not. Treat them with respect where they live, and do what needs to be done to keep the peace with them. Know their makeup and their personality, and then respect their boundaries and limitations.

How Do You Discern It?

You may be wondering how you can recognize and identify these things. How do you discern where someone is living? As you gain experience in relationships, you will find your way and see that some things work and others don't. This is all a part of the trial-and-error process of getting to know people and their unique ways.

One of the best ways to develop and demonstrate respect for others is not only to listen to their words, but also to listen to their heart. Give them the opportunity to completely share their heart with you. Allow them time to speak, and then engage in such a way that helps direct them to the specifics at hand. This type of communication helps foster stronger and better relationships.

Building Good Relationships

Building good relationships is important for our communities, and so it should be embraced. Get attached or reattached to others. It will take work to be a valuable player on the team, for it doesn't happen overnight. Keep a team consciousness before you, and work to be part of that team.

You don't have to agree on every detail to work together. In some instances, it may be good to agree to disagree, allowing time to think things over. Then you can discuss it again at some later date.

This kind of attitude toward relationships ensures that when something unexpected happens, you will not be taken by surprise. You must learn how to give people time and room to grow. Even when iniquity, sins and accidents happen (and they tend to come at the most unpredictable and unfortunate seasons in relationships), have patience with those involved. Our heavenly Father loves everyone and will not give up on anyone. He offers salvation for all those who come to Him, and He will not cast them away. You should display this same heart and attitude toward others. If you show compassion toward them, you will receive compassion yourself.

Accidents and sins tend to come at the most unpredictable and unfortunate seasons in relationships!

Hurt and Out of Touch?

Maybe you have been hurt and out of touch with someone for a season. Now is the time to come out of hibernation and get back into the real game of life. Don't prolong the process while waiting to be healed. Repent for having allowed something to hinder your relationship in the first place, pick yourself up, move forward and recover all. It is time to engage, engage and engage some more.

God's Word teaches us:

The sacrifices of God are a broken spirit: a broken and a contrite heart, O God, thou wilt not despise. Psalm 51:17

Accidents and sins are a certainly, so don't expect those around you to be perfect. Accept them as they are.

Discussion Questions for Chapter 2
"Accidents and Sins Are a Certainty"

NAME: _____

DATE: _____

1. In light of the fact that accidents and sins are a certainty, is there something you have been holding against yourself that you need to release?

   _____
   _____
   _____
   _____
   _____

2. Are there people you need to forgive for having sinned against you? If so, who?

   _____
   _____
   _____
   _____
   _____

*Remember, forgiveness frees you and it releases God to make all things work together for your good (see Romans 8:28).

3. **Ponder this: Are you ready to open your heart to foster new relationships, understanding that none of us is exempt from accidents and sins, but that we are required to forgive others and trust God that He will show us how to dwell with others according to knowledge (see 1 Peter 3:7)?**

_____

_____

_____

_____

_____

— Your Reflections —

CHAPTER 3

Beyond the Womb

Many, O LORD my God, are thy wonderful works which thou hast done, and thy thoughts which are to us-ward: they cannot be reckoned up in order unto thee: if I would declare and speak of them, they are more than can be numbered. Psalm 40:5

I will praise thee; for I am fearfully and wonderfully made: marvellous are thy works; and that my soul knoweth right well. Psalm 139:14

Sometimes it is hard for us to think outside the box because we have been programmed to think inside the box. This programming began when we were still in the womb. Even there, we began forming thoughts, expressions and, yes, considering limitations.

> *We were affected by our mother's pains, her feelings, her every thought and the labor she had to endure to give us birth!*

Affected by Our Mother's Pains

Through the miracle of conception, each of us was formed inside the womb of a woman, and I cannot think of a better way for us to have arrived here on this earth. But in the process we were affected by our mother's pains, her feelings, her every thought and the labor she had to endure to give us birth. These were all part of the process of our development. During the months your mother carried you, everything in her world had the ability to affect your personality, your particular makeup and your future development.

But there is a breaking out of the box that is near for those who will dare to go beyond their mother's womb. You see, the womb was never made to hold us permanently; it was only meant to be transitional. Just as we need to get out of the box, we are all called to break out of the old and into something new. What I'm referring to is the *alpha* and *omega* of our lives.

The Alpha and Omega of Our Lives

No one knows what their next relationship may bring or when it will end. The potential for what can develop from a single relationship is endless. There is a beginning and an end that bring relationships into a higher dimension of potential. Breaking out of the box is like bursting out of your mother's womb. At the point of birth, the future was out of your control in some respects, but it eventually became your responsibility to reach for it. This made it an *alpha* and *omega*, with new beginnings and many endings. When you understand the dynamics of relationships, the journey becomes exciting.

Early Adversity Taught Me

Early on in my own life, adversity was present, but through it I learned valuable lessons that

I could not have learned in any other way. At the age of five, for example, I was diagnosed with a scalp disease that prevented me from starting school until the infection could be treated and cured. What was interesting is that I had a mother who believed that I was destined for greatness and refused to let my illness box me in or allow me to feel sorry for myself. Instead, she made our time together priceless.

Looking back, I can honestly say that Mom was my best teacher. Our mother-and-son relationship proved to be the seed that inspired something awesome in my future. In between my trips to the hospital, she decided to sit me in front of a piano and teach me how to play. In this way, at that young age, I began learning to play the piano, and by the time I was eight, I was already advertising for one of the major music stores in the mall. This experience was my *alpha*. What a great beginning it was!

By the age of twelve, I was playing with a band, and by thirteen I was performing professionally. Not long after that, I began to travel and perform. Between the ages of fifteen and eighteen, I toured the country and worked with some of the greatest musicians and bands (Clarence

Carter, James Brown, Chocolate Milk and Wet Paint — just to name a few).

I Credit My Mother

In view of my humble beginnings, I credit my musical success to my mother. She responded to my illness by thinking outside of the box. She wouldn't settle for defeat.

You see, to move beyond the womb is to believe that failure is not an option. Dare to be greater than the obstacles that try to block you. It's time to think of greatness, and adversity can be the friend who gets you there.

God Has a Plan for You

God has a plan for you. He said to Jeremiah:

Before I formed thee in the belly I knew thee; and before thou camest forth out of the womb I sanctified thee, and I ordained thee a prophet unto the nations. Jeremiah 1:5

The truth is that the spirit of a man exists before the womb. Our spirits came from somewhere or Someone other than our parents. As for our bodies, naked we came into the world and naked we will leave it (see Job 1:21). Getting out of the box challenges us to reconsider our values, and when we do, material things suddenly become less important to us. The only thing we can bring with us beyond this life is relationship.

This shows us that in everything we do on this earth we must have a beyond-the-womb and even a beyond-death mentality. Therefore, emphasis should be placed on the need to have valued relationships based on eternal purposes. Beyond-the-womb thinking develops relationships that far exceed the natural limitations imposed on us by the birth given to us by our parents and far exceed any present circumstances that would seem to limit us. This presents us with the opportunity for our life's legacy to continue on for generations after our short life on earth has expired.

Break Out of the Box

We can break out of the box and experience the supreme love and acceptance of the heavenly Father. He loves us, regardless of prejudices, hurts, pains, unforgiveness, misunderstandings, bad decisions or unfortunate circumstances due to the womb's limitations. Even before we were born, God knew each of us and ordained something great for us. We all came from God's great bosom of purpose and will return to eternity. Now, however, we are given time, in this process called *life*, for personal development and for building quality relationships.

God's Thoughts of You Are All Good

God said through the prophet Jeremiah:

> *For I know the thoughts that I think toward you, saith the* Lord, *thoughts of peace, and not of evil, to give you an expected end.*   Jeremiah 29:11

In everything we do on this earth we must have a beyond-the-womb and even a beyond-death mentality!

God's thoughts for us are all good, thoughts that will bring us to *"an expected end."* We were placed on earth to receive His thoughts, express them and connect with others. The choice to live beyond the womb is to model His love for others. His will is that people from every nation, kingdom and tribe live as Christ lived and, thus, bring the hope of glory to the earth. In this respect, neither religion, nationality, skin color, nor social or economic status matter. God loves us all the same.

Living beyond the womb means that nothing is impossible for him who believes (see Mark 9:23 and Luke 1:37). Every soul that breathes has value, and to relate to others is to value their soul. Life is God's gift to you; what you do with your life and how you help others are your gifts back to Him.

In his Revelation, John saw this:

And they sung a new song, saying, Thou art worthy to take the book, and to open the seals thereof: for thou wast slain, and hast redeemed us to God by thy blood out of every kindred, and tongue, and people, and nation.

Revelation 5:9

Get a broader vision of life. Move out of the womb and its limitations, be the person God destined you to be, and help others to do the same. That's what relationship is all about.

Discussion Questions for Chapter 3
"Beyond the Womb"

NAME: _____

DATE: _____

1. What traits, shortcomings, benefits or blessings do you see in yourself that have passed to you from your mother's womb (your family bloodline)?

_____

_____

_____

_____

_____

2. Have you ever felt boxed in by your family's expectations or limitations? Discuss this.

_____

_____

_____

_____

_____

3. Are you ready to enlarge your territory by getting out of the box to explore the endless opportunities that God has prepared for you beyond the womb (beyond the familiar things)?

_____

_____

_____

_____

_____

4. In what ways can you use adversity to your advantage?

_____

_____

_____

_____

_____

— Your Reflections —

Getting Some Sense

Jesus said unto him, Thou shalt love the LORD thy God with all thy heart, and with all thy soul, and with all thy mind.
 And the second is like unto it, Thou shalt love thy neighbour as thyself.

Matthew 22:37 and 39

By now you should be ready to embrace my purpose for writing this book. If you have read the first three chapters and have made it this far, let me congratulate you for staying the course.

What I call "getting some sense" is pivotal, both for change and for awakening your gifts, talents and deep treasures for a more accurate assessment of relationships. You may ask: "What do you mean by 'getting some sense'?" I mean adding fire to your passion and investing first in yourself. It all starts with an inner voice saying, "I have a purpose; I have a destiny." This passion becomes clearer when the commitment to getting some sense is primary in your plans for reaching your desired goals.

Ask Yourself the Right Questions

Asking yourself the right questions will move you toward your purpose. You might ask yourself:

- Who am I?
- Why am I here?
- What is my purpose?
- What must I do to position myself for my destiny?

Let me say again: *The Foundation for Purpose Is Relationship.* Therefore, whatever purpose you have in life, it will take relationships to get you there.

Have you heard the familiar cliche: It is not *what* you know but *who* you know? Relationships can determine what doors are opened to you and what doors are closed to you. So it's time to get some sense.

Everything in life happens as a result of relationships. However, the most important relationship is with yourself. How do you accept yourself? And are you taking responsibility to become the best person you can be?

Just as the foundation for purpose is relationship, the same holds true for its destruction. With whom are you involved? What kinds of people are attracted to you and what kinds of people do you associate with? Aside from these relationships, any possible self-destruction or breakdown is connected to how you relate to yourself.

> *Asking yourself the right questions will move you toward your purpose!*

- Do you speak positive or negative thoughts to yourself?
- Do you take care of your physical body?
- Do you exercise and eat the foods necessary to maximize your strength?
- Do you take time to rest, have fun and enjoy life?

You Must First Value Yourself

To value others in relationships, you must first value yourself. You can't love someone else more than you love yourself. You cannot give something you don't possess. Therefore, it is unwise to put more into other relationships without having first taken the time to invest in yourself.

This is plain and reasonable to see. You don't have to be a rocket scientist in order to have some good sense. *"Love thy God,"* Jesus said, *"and love thy neighbor AS THYSELF."* So getting some sense means that it's time to have a good relationship with yourself.

Take Actions to Invest in Yourself

Do you take actions to invest in yourself? For my part, I recently attended an educational training at Applied Scholastic International. On the first day, I was exposed to two profound yet simple thoughts that made an impact on me. The first was that study means "to look at something, ask about it and read about it." The second was that "a person cannot learn unless he has the desire and the will to learn." The process of getting some sense begins with wanting to learn and taking the initiative to study. Jesus said:

> *And I say unto you, Ask, and it shall be given you; seek, and ye shall find; knock, and it shall be opened unto you. For every one that asketh receiveth; and he that seeketh findeth; and to him that knocketh it shall be opened.*
>
> Luke 11:9-10

Those who get some sense will awaken to find their overall quality of life improved because they have valued themselves enough to invest in their future. Those who fail to get some sense will continue to be co-dependent, making themselves a nuisance in all their relationships. This is equivalent to living your life riding on the backs of others, not daring to trust your own blessings, talents and abilities.

On the other hand, there are those who take the initiative to ask because *"it shall be given,"* to seek and keep on seeking until they find, to knock and keep on knocking until the door opens to them.

Do Whatever You Need to Do

Getting some sense means going back to school if necessary, taking classes to improve your self-image and becoming more confident in life. Take a trip. Explore your interests. Revisit your field of dreams. Write down your vision and set some new goals.

> *Look ahead, set your expectations beyond your current limitations, and ask for help!*

If need be, get a personal trainer for your physical needs. At a minimum, engage yourself in healthy exercises such as walking, running, biking or swimming. Take time for medical checkups, including regular dental visits. Be alert. Don't take your most prized possession for granted.

By the way, that prized possession is you. So you need to take better care of yourself. Make wiser choices. Turn off the television and read, study and learn — for your own peace of mind.

"I Can't Afford It"

You might say, "We are experiencing hard times, so I can't afford to do all of that. So what do I do?" You may find yourself in a place where you don't have resources to take care of yourself — not enough to afford proper insurance, not enough to eat more healthy foods — or your spirit may be so broken that you can't find the will to take care of yourself. What do you do in that case?

May I suggest that you look ahead, set your expectations beyond your current limitations, and ask for help. There is always hope, so don't give up, and never stop expecting things to get better. Just the fact that you have breath in your body is a sign that life is not over for you.

It is important to begin with valuing your life and believing that there is a God who really cares. He specializes in hard situations and circumstances and does His best work when all seems lost and gone.

Getting some sense gives each of us the ability to believe that things will change. The initial change is choosing to take on a different attitude. Nothing has the power to take away your ability and free will to believe that things can improve in your life.

Sometimes you may need to ask others for help, even though you don't want to. The truth is that embarrassment and pride are only counterfeiters clothed in false humility. They keep us from obtaining what we really need. When we share with others what we are going through, pride is dethroned, and the feeling of embarrassment becomes a stepping-stone to building stronger relationships. This is crucial.

Jesus taught:

> *Judge not, and ye shall not be judged: condemn not, and ye shall not be condemned: forgive, and ye shall be forgiven.*　　　　Luke 6:37

For centuries now the church has mistakenly taught that we should care for others more than we care for ourselves. This mind-set was probably due to ignorance or the fear of people becoming prideful or selfish. These days we can have a healthier and balanced perspective in both the natural and the spiritual.

The proper relationship between us and God and has a lot to do with how we invest in ourselves. As I said before, we cannot give something we don't have, and therefore, we have to learn how to give and also how to receive.

Stop Judging and Condemning Yourself

The first thing we must do is stop judging and condemning ourselves so harshly. Let the Creator be the final Judge. Forgive yourself. You can never move forward by holding on to your past. Believe me, I know what I'm talking about.

Before I truly came to understand God's love and mercy, I had actually become an atheist, one who did not believe in the existence of God at all. I did not want to face my own sins, and it was always easier to blame someone else for what was going wrong in my life. The problem was not that God didn't love me, but that I didn't love the person I had become.

By the age of nineteen, I was already abusing drugs. And, before long, I was depressed, suicidal and had lost my grip on life. I was moving from relationship to relationship, still empty inside. I had material things — money, sex and drugs — but I was very unhappy.

If there is a God, I thought, *how could He allow so much pain in one person's life?* The biggest problem was that I refused to forgive myself for the awful things I had done, and so I had no hope for a better future. Then, by an act of mercy, God spared my life when I should have died. This proved to be the turning point for me, for getting some sense. It was a great wake-up call which gave me faith and the chance to forgive others, myself and — yes — even God.

You Must Learn to Forgive

God gives each of us our own free will, and before you can love and receive love, you must learn to forgive. He doesn't force any of us to forgive. We have to choose to do it. For me, it proved to be the most important thing, one that would open the door to genuine relationships.

The first step to getting some sense is forgiving ourselves, but, for me, forgiveness provided the platform for building new relationships, beginning with my relationship with the Creator Himself. It was my time to be honest about my condition and give myself something I desperately needed

– self-forgiveness. Then I was able to forgive others. Jesus taught us:

Give, and it shall be given unto you; good measure, pressed down, and shaken together, and running over, shall men give into your bosom. For with the same measure that ye mete withal it shall be measured to you again.

Luke 6:38

I have never seen a farmer taking seeds from his own stock and planting them in his neighbor's fields. Farmers sow their seed in their own fields, and then they wait for a harvest so that they can invest in others. Taking the time to plan and invest in yourself and doing the right thing with what you have in your hands positions you to develop and maintain good relationships.

By an act of mercy, God spared my life when I should have died!

There is joy when you invest in yourself, not for selfish ambitions, but in order to have an abundance to give to others. This prepares you for quality relationships, and for what we now call networking and synergy.

Integrity is about becoming whole and being honest with yourself. No one else can live your life or your vision. So don't play games with your life, trying to please others, and risk missing your destiny.

If your vision requires you to relocate, do it. If you need to change jobs, do it. If you just need to take a break, do it. Don't be afraid to do what you need to do.

Training for a new career will cost you. It will require research and finding creative ways of studying and learning. The Internet is available to us today, so use it. Take time each week to work on your personal projects, and always remember to pay yourself before paying others. Prepare your containers for good relationships, pressed down and running over, to be added unto you.

Now you are ready for The Secret of God's Power.

Discussion Questions for Chapter 4
"Getting Some Sense"

NAME: _____

DATE: _____

1. What is the meaning of the phrase *getting some sense*? (See pages 63 and 64).

   _____
   _____
   _____
   _____
   _____

2. What will you do now to invest in yourself?

   _____
   _____
   _____
   _____
   _____

3. As an act of self-realization, share something you like about yourself. (Take at least one minute).

_____

_____

_____

_____

_____

4. What clues do your gifts give you concerning your future?

_____

_____

_____

_____

_____

5. How can loving yourself prepare you for new relationships?

_____

_____

_____

_____

— Your Reflections —

CHAPTER 5

The Secret of God's Power

Wisdom is the principal thing; therefore get wisdom: and with all thy getting get understanding.   Proverbs 4:7

Getting some sense is a prerequisite for opening doors to new relationships and experiencing the awesome power of God's love. A given individual may be a door for us, and every relationship has the potential of being a door to something we have never experienced or somewhere we have never been before. After getting some sense, we must then leave the familiar and begin to share our gifts, talents and knowledge with others. This type of exposure will foster a new frontier of relationships.

We Cannot Just Assume

If we never venture out and connect with others, we cannot assume that people are somehow aware of our gifts, talents, knowledge or wisdom. Making the connection is important, and that requires skill, patience, time and a good attitude.

> *We cannot assume that people are somehow aware of our gifts, talents, knowledge or wisdom!*

We also need to develop the art of knowing when and how to use the doors God puts in our lives. First, let's establish two major principles that work hand-in-hand to pull it all together:

The Two Major Principles

The first principle is our title: *"The Foundation for Purpose Is Relationship,"* and the second principle is this: "The Secret of God's Power Is Timing." I firmly believe that the secret of God's power is in the right timing, and I will be expounding upon this concept in greater detail in a sequel to this book. Let me say here that right timing is a moment divinely given which sets the stage for interacting with others, to turn pivotal corners in life. If we blunder with the proper timing, we could potentially jeopardize every blessing, benefit and opportunity in this season of relationships.

Should another opportunity present itself, we must hope and pray that we are adequately prepared to engage. Only God knows what will pass our way again. For some, there is a one-time missed opportunity, while others seem to be given countless occasions to rectify and reclaim their position. Since we can never know for sure which will be the case with us, wisdom advises us to be prepared at all times and to act at the opportune moment.

What Right Timing Means

I must repeat this principle again: **The secret of God's power is timing**. Timing means being in the right place at the right moment with the right motives in our hearts. This is the formula for releasing God's glory, and when we reach this place, there will be a sense of confidence and empowerment in our relationships. Timing will test every motive in our hearts and weed out excess baggage from past experiences. God's true glory is revealed when we walk in personal integrity in our authentic self at His appointed time.

Since timing is so important and time is so precious, we can never take lightly the people who cross our paths. Be ready to adjust or change directions to embrace the appropriate season. If our motives are right and we are prepared, we will not miss the timing.

When we have genuine motives concerning the well-being of others, we are ready for the secret of God's power. Once we arrive at this place, we will be amazed as one new interaction unfolds after another, releasing phenomenal relationships, beyond our greatest dreams.

You Won't Have to Manipulate

When you are operating and flowing in God's power, you won't have to manipulate, scheme or control people to get their attention. In fact, just the opposite will be true. Your destiny will begin to take shape before your very eyes. You will be set on course to connect with the right people in the right place at the right time. All of this will happen because you are learning to have full confidence in your authentic self. Since you now know how to relate to yourself, improve yourself and celebrate yourself, you are ready to embrace others.

At this point, relationships are no longer a need and a burden, but, rather, a blessing. Having them is no longer a hassle; it is now a thrill. This is more than an assignment; it is your choice. It is beyond how you feel; it is your will. So reach out, give a hand up, fellowship with others and, in the process, build new relationships. Your best days are just ahead, so go for it. And, as you go for it, don't be afraid to miss it!

Learning to Accept Setbacks

One of the greatest challenges of embracing the proper timing is learning to accept setbacks. They will come in even the greatest relationships, but you can still maintain peace within. This kind of peace can only be experienced when tragedies occur and you feel their hardest blows. There is an old saying: "When it rains, it pours," and it's true. There is an extraordinary grace and power hidden in a reserved chamber of your spirit that is only available and can only be released at the right time. God's power is often released after there has been a setback, which then becomes a set-up with the purpose of you experiencing a greater comeback.

Many times it seems that we are just arriving at our destination when God allows a tragedy or unfortunate crisis to occur. This often appears to us, at the beginning, at least, to be very painful, but if we stick with the course, the ultimate outcome will be of far greater benefit.

My Awesome Mother

Let me share here another story about my awesome mother. She reared me and my siblings by doing domestic work — sewing, ironing and doing housekeeping for wealthy families. Then, as I approached my teen years, she started working in a sewing factory, making men's ties. She had to walk miles to get a bus to work and then walk back home miles from the bus stop in the evening. Some days she struggled to make it home after a hard day's labor.

One dreary evening Mom came home so late that we began to worry if perhaps she had been in an accident or something else bad had happened to her. When she finally did arrive, she didn't look like her normal self, and it was very obvious to me that she was gravely ill. She soon made arrangements to get to a hospital, for her very life was in jeopardy. She had suffered a stroke.

I can never forget what we children felt while Mom was in the hospital. It was a feeling of deep loss. She was our world.

When doctors released Mom from the hospital, they gave her a very bleak report. She had little or no hope of recovering fully from the

Many times it seems that we are just arriving at our destination when God allows a tragedy or unfortunate crisis to occur!

stroke, they said. What's more, family and friends who visited her were already pronouncing a death sentence over her life. It seemed that our mother was going down for the count. She was told, in no uncertain terms, that she must set her house in order, for she would not live long. Amazingly, it was those closest to Mom who spoke the most negative and hurtful things to her.

God Had a Plan

But God had a plan in all of this. Those people didn't know that Mom's season of crisis was positioning her for the greatest future she could ever have dreamed of for herself. One day, while she was lying there on her sick bed, she got an idea — a revelation of sorts. She had been doing a lot of thinking, a lot of soul searching. It might be difficult for her in the days ahead to do the manual labor she had been doing for years, but she still had a mind to think. Domestic work was what she was familiar with, but she was willing to make a change.

Mom believed and trusted that deep within her there was still a purpose. So, guess what happened out of that apparent end-of-life crisis that had taken her by surprise? She said to herself, "I must get out of this bed and get back to work. I may not be able to do heavy housework for someone else or even work in the factory, but I can work." In that moment she put the factory behind her and set out on a journey to pursue a more rewarding career. Her faith had moved her to a new place. She might not be able to do a lot of things, but there was one thing she excelled at.

Mom Became a Successful Piano Teacher

What was Mom's new idea? It was to teach piano lessons, and she was good at it. That idea so inspired her that she literally sprang from her bed and began to advertise her services and look for paying pupils. At first, there was just one student, but even in her crippled state, Mom faithfully taught that one student.

Before long, one student had become two, two had become four, four had become ten, and ten had become hundreds. Mom went on to help many who had only dreamed of learning to play music. As this enlarged and expanded edition of the book goes to press, she is eighty-six, and she still enjoys teaching. Many of her former students went on to become fine upstanding citizens, and now their children are taking music lessons from her.

Allow Adversity to Become Your Friend

It is exciting when we can allow adversity to become our friend and to catapult us to a new place of destiny. By digging deep within, my mother taught me that if you believe you can recover from whatever life throws your way. Because of her faith in God, Mom moved from doing domestic work to being the boss of her own future. This also taught me the powerful lesson revealed in the next chapter: Don't be afraid, even if you seem to have missed it!

Discussion Questions for Chapter 5
"The Secret of God's Power"

NAME: _____

DATE: _____

1. How often do you share your gifts, talents or
   knowledge with others? Explain.

   _____
   _____
   _____
   _____
   _____

2. What are some ways that you can venture
   out and connect with others?

   _____
   _____
   _____
   _____
   _____

3. How have your past seasons of pain prepared you for Gods greater purpose?

_____

_____

_____

_____

_____

— Your Reflections —

CHAPTER 6

When You've Missed It

Rejoice not against me, O mine enemy: when I fall, I shall arise; when I sit in darkness, the LORD shall be a light unto me.   Micah 7:8

As we come closer to the turning point of the book, this chapter may well be your most treasured. Misunderstandings, abuses, betrayals, separations and even divorces should not rob you of your God-given purpose in life. Even if you add to the list your personal mistakes, don't allow them to derail your future.

It Was Not Meant to Be Your End

Whatever may have happened to bring pain into your life, it was not meant to be your end, but, rather, the platform or the launching pad to a new beginning. Great things are still possible, as long as you have the gift of breath in your body and a will to live. You can arise and recover from despair or any kind of set-back and finish stronger than ever.

It is not what, how, why or when things happen that makes relationships sour. Rather, it is what you give permission to in your heart that matters most. Will you become bitter or better? Paralyzed or mobilized? One who is separated from life or one who is reconnected with life? Will you sit as a sideline observer or choose to become an active participant in the game of life? Will you continue to be upset at the other players or will you choose to become the play-maker?

Three Different Types of Characters

Everyone who chooses to make a difference in life has three different types of characters assigned to their journey. There are those who love you no matter what happens. There are those who are always trying to tell you how to live your life, for they love and are sometimes addicted to

micro-management. The most trying relationships, however, are with those you trusted and
they betrayed you.

It Nearly Devastated My Life

One such experience nearly devastated my
life. I shared some impor-
tant information with friends
about things I was struggling
with, and later they used this
knowledge to bring hurtful
accusations against me. I had
a choice: Would I become
bitter? Or would I become a
better person? Simply put, I
needed to find a place in my
heart to forgive them. It was
imperative that I move on,
without feeling victimized
by those who had lacked true integrity.

> *Will*
> *you*
> *become*
> *bitter*
> *or*
> *better?*
> *Paralyzed*
> *or*
> *mobilized?*

After struggling with the desire to prove my
innocence, I settled the issue by deciding that
some things are not worth defending to those
who are not willing to listen. I realized that if
the heart of a person is still closed, after a sincere

effort to resolve an issue, perhaps to continue this relationship was not for me. From that day until now, I have grown to understand that a sour relationship does not determine who I am. Instead of feeling like a victim because of betrayal, I possess the power to move on and soar in new relationships. This experience taught me an important lesson: I don't have to withdraw from trusting people. If I accommodate the blows with confidence and without reacting, but rather responding with love and respect, I can expect a favorable outcome. It's all my choice.

Betrayal Can Become a Bridge Over Troubled Waters

Who knew that betrayal could become a bridge over troubled waters, to help me cross over from my past to my future? It provided an opportunity for me to enlarge my capacity by working with others. And so life goes on.

Can you swallow your pride and admit that regardless of who is right, you have the opportunity to recover and be restored? Everyone has issues, but making the appropriate decisions about them can free and empower you. Reaching the point of not reacting and, instead, responding appropriately will take hard work, focus, patience and practice. Regardless of your pain, disappointment or fear, displaying anger will not contribute either to your peace or your destiny.

Think about this, and don't be surprised by it. The action of those closest to you in relationship can awaken the need to change your ways. All of the emotional outbursts that follow when you miss it represent an honest and new opportunity for the hole in the soul to be maturely dealt with.

Relationships that Malfunction

I have two things to share about relationships that malfunction:

1. Betrayal is a possibility that comes with character growth. You won't know true loss until you have been betrayed by someone you have chosen to love. As painful as it may be, eventually you will recover and decide to trust again. There is always a risk of betrayal in relationships.

2. Rejection is inevitable, a certainty in everyone's life. This plays a major part in our

If you choose to love anyone more than you love God and yourself, you're missing the purpose of relationships!

learning to grow up. The underlying outcome is that you experience the Father's acceptance as your Creator. He allows you to be rejected by people so that you can find His acceptance, which is greater than any man or woman can offer.

This process, therefore, along with other painful experiences in life, will protect us from empowering people and making them our earthly idols. If you choose to love anyone more than you love God and yourself, you're missing the purpose of relationships. You are overly empowering others rather than embracing and walking in the power of the Father.

Power Is Delegated Authority

Power is delegated authority. This means that whatever power a person has, it has been given to him by someone else. In relationships, we give people the power to speak into our lives, affect our lives and encourage or discourage us. Jesus said:

Behold, I give unto you power to tread on serpents and scorpions, and over all the power of the enemy: and nothing shall by any means hurt you.   Luke 10:19

God has given us the *"power to tread on serpents and scorpions"* and *"over all the power of the enemy."* And His promise is: *"nothing shall by any means hurt you."* When you've missed it and people you call your friends display the character of a snake or a scorpion, don't allow that to be a fatal blow that knocks you so far down that you refuse to get up and try again. You can overcome it.

Micah warned his enemies:

Rejoice not against me, O mine enemy: when I fall, I shall arise; when I sit in darkness, the LORD shall be a light unto me.   Micah 7:8

Psalm 91:2 says

I will say of the LORD, He is my refuge and my fortress: my God; in him will I trust.

Your will and choice to live on are greater than the attacks that may try to keep you down. There is a strength that comes with trusting God. Remember, God has a secret place for you. Hear this: purpose in life is bigger than man's misfortune, mistakes, disappointments and sins. When disappointments come, the sooner we can get over our pride and the feeling of shame, the sooner we will be ready for the best that can come out of that failure.

Dealing with Your Pride

For those of us who love God, the way up is the way down, so now let's talk about pride and how to deal with it. Pride is the number one enemy of your recovery time. A part of life is that you will sometimes miss it in relationships. Developing a mind-set to never fall backward when things go wrong but to look ahead and move beyond your past is wisdom that will propel you into your destiny.

Learn to enrich yourself for your future by gaining new momentum by falling forward. Take every relationship problem as an opportunity to become better prepared and equipped for the challenging days ahead. It has been said that the definition of insanity is to keep doing the same thing over and over, expecting a different result.

Let Go and Meditate on It

Letting go of the need to control others, combined with the ability to sit and be still are vital to the process of what you can learn from your mistakes. After missing it, you will need time to meditate, reflect and revamp some of your ways with relationships. This is not a bad thing, and it's not the end of life. It is, rather, the beginning of a new season.

Some people can be dangerous because of the toxic waste they carry in the unhealed areas of their mind. You may also be toxic and may need time to detoxify your own heart. Humility will forever come before true honor. King David said:

It is good for me that I have been afflicted; that I might learn thy statutes. Psalm 119:71

Respect the Principles Governing Relationships

Relationships have principles that must be honored in order to work. Being humbled through brokenness should awaken us to being less assuming and controlling of others. Don't always feel that you have to take charge of everything. Release people and stop fearing and worrying about what is going to happen to you or them. Instead, trust God for the best outcome. Stay away from micro-management.

Avoid a Slave Mentality

Avoid a slave mentality. A slave mentality is when you are not willing to let go and trust others to do the right thing, based on their personal convictions. Moses came out of Egypt, but the ways of Egypt still had some negative influence on his life. He felt that he had to do everything to make things work. That was a slave mentality.

A slave mentality reflects the concept of a pyramid business. There is one person at the top, and everyone else falls below him. Under this system, your success depends on what you can get out of your workers, rather than what you can contribute to their success. Rather than a team working together, it's a ruling monarchy.

Build a Team Concept

Building good re-lationships will take a heart to work as one:

T ogether
E ach
A ccomplishes
M uch

Being humbled through brokenness should awaken us to being less assuming and controlling of others!

When we develop a team mind-set, we rec-ognize that others can and will overcome their own demons. Their gifts, talents and abilities will improve when you allow patience to have its perfect work (see James 1:4).

Things to Avoid

Keeping it real means taking responsibility for the past without stifling your future relationships. Let me assure you that there will be many other opportunities for new relationships, so don't blow it by being conceited or over-familiar. Manipulation, self-righteousness, debating issues and using scare tactics and threats are great ways to destroy relationships. Stay away from these offensive devices as much as possible.

The apostle Paul said: "I will not eat meat, if it offends my brother" (see Romans 14:21). What kind of love is that? There are some things that we can avoid, if we know our boundaries, stay in our own lane and mind our own business. Love will help us navigate our hearts to stop speaking with emotions that deeply offend others.

The Scriptures teach us:

A man that hath friends must shew himself friendly: and there is a friend that sticketh closer than a brother.   Proverbs 18:24

Indeed, we all make many mistakes. For if we could control our tongues, we would be perfect and could also control ourselves in every other way. James 3:2, NLT

When you have missed it, pick yourself up, dust yourself off, and get ready for the future. Your best days are just ahead.

Discussion Questions for Chapter 6
"When You've Missed It"

NAME: _____

DATE: _____

1. How have prior relationships launched you into new relationships of purpose?

   _____
   _____
   _____
   _____
   _____

2. Have your past relationships made you better or bitter? Do you currently see new relationships as opportunities or liabilities? Be honest with yourself.

   _____
   _____
   _____
   _____
   _____

3. What nuggets of wisdom have you gained from challenging relationships?

_____

_____

_____

_____

_____

4. What are some of your ways that may need to be revamped to build new relationships and strengthen existing ones?

_____

_____

_____

_____

_____

5. How can you apply the team concept to your relationships with others? Explain

_____

_____

_____

_____

— Your Reflections —

CHAPTER 7

Taking Personal Responsibility

And David said, What have I now done? Is there not a cause?   1 Samuel 17:29

Let me begin this chapter with the story of a seventeen-year-old boy who was destined to become king over a great nation. As a boy, however, he was excluded from family affairs because he was considered to be a half-breed. While the family did other things, he was given menial labor in a far field, so that he was hidden from the public.

He Could Not Change the Facts of His Conception

The boy could not change the time of his conception, the place of his birth, his skin color

> Although this young man was considered to be the black sheep of his family, there was something special and authentic that had been placed in him by God Himself!

or his social-economic status. These were already in place when he arrived. He couldn't say from his mother's womb, "I don't want to be born of this woman or be a part of this family. I don't approve of their religious beliefs or their position in life. I want out of this plan." You see, we're all born into relationships in which we have no choice in the matter.

Although this young man was considered to be the black sheep of his family, there was something special and authentic that had been placed in him by God Himself. Deep inside the inner workings of his heart and soul was a cry that, when faced with confrontation, would launch him into his assigned purpose in life.

The Setting

A ferocious giant, skilled in weaponry, threatened the nation and challenged its warriors to a duel. One of the opposing soldiers, a group of soldiers or even a brigade could have accepted this challenge and taken the responsibility, but none of them were willing to do it. No one, not even the most skilled warriors among them, moved to face down the giant and save the nation.

Then, to everyone's amazement, a rather small, ruddy teenage boy stepped up to the plate, took responsibility and accepted the challenge. He understood the threat and refused to stand by and do nothing while his people were humiliated. In his innocence and with great integrity, he proclaimed: *"What have I now done? Is there not a cause?"* He was taking personal responsibility.

The "Solitary" Have Purpose

God's Word declares:

God setteth the solitary in families: he bringeth out those which are bound with chains: but the rebellious dwell in a dry land.   Psalm 68:6

God places people who are different from everyone else, *"the solitary,"* in families. These individuals are loners, and they often face life's problems alone. But solitary individuals, because of their blessings and obedience, are in a unique position to help their families. Such was the case with this particular seventeen-year-old boy, who would later become the great King David.

When David took personal responsibility for defeating Goliath, the path to the throne was paved. An entire nation benefited from his courage. And his family was blessed because he refused to allow the circumstances of his birth to define him. He could not change those circumstances, but he could determine his fate in life.

God Designed Goliath Just for David

God designed the giant Goliath just for David. This was his personal assignment, to take on this particular challenge at this particular time. And he did it alone.

When the moment arrived to make a decision, David didn't have time or opportunity to discuss the situation with anyone else. He had to make a decision, and the decision he made would change his life forever. At seventeen, this one event paved a new pathway for David for future relationships.

Is there not a cause? David made it his personal responsibility to do something about a problem that would not go away. He obeyed his heart. And just as with David, obedience is your key too.

Obedience Is the Key

"Obedience to what?" you might ask. Obedience to the call from inside your belly that cries, *"Is there not a cause?"* You hear the call during the night when others are sleeping and in the morning when you awake. It just won't go away. Deep inside, you know things can be better. You know that you are supposed to go further than your grandparents, your mother, father, aunts and uncles. Make a decision that their suffering will not have been in vain.

What have you done? Is there not a cause? Someone has to cross over to pave the way for others. Someone has to accomplish more than previous generations. Someone in your bloodline has to be the first to get their bachelors, masters, MBA or PhD. Someone has to start their own business, write books, travel overseas or take a mission trip. In short, it's time to get a life. If you're still breathing, it's not too late! As Kimberly DeAnn Williamson, one of my spiritual daughters, wrote in her book of poetry entitled *Mountain, Move*: "It ain't over until God says it's over!" [1]

You have probably asked yourself or others the questions:

"Why me?"

"Why do I have to take the lead?"

"Why should the responsibility of being the solitary one be on me?"

The simple answer is: Why not you? *Is there not a cause?*

Saul's Advice Was Inaccurate

Even King Saul, an expert, gave David inaccurate advice, but David concluded that the giant would fall, and it was his responsibility to make it happen. He knew that with God on his side, the giant would be defeated, and his head would be cut off. David's mind-set was not shaped by others. It was an inner cry and a willingness to be responsible for it. His relationship with God and himself superseded his relationship with men, and so his life was catapulted into another dimension of purpose and

1. Self-published: 2008

relationship. Having a cause and sticking to it will grace us with the wisdom and ability to responsibly navigate relationships.

The last part of Psalm 68:6 speaks of *"the rebellious"* dwelling *"in a dry land."* The longer we avoid the responsibility of our true calling and purpose in life, the longer we will be unfruitful and miss the experience of true joy. Many have accepted a life with limitations because they chose to ignore that taking responsibility for our behavior and actions each day positions us to live a life without personal blame, with less distractions and a clearer direction for our future.

Always keep this question in mind, *"Is there not a cause?"* This will help you to complete one assignment at a time. Narrow your options

Having a cause and sticking to it will grace us with the wisdom and ability to responsibly navigate relationships!

and start building for success and significance. Think about future generations and about leaving them a rich legacy. This will speak louder when we are gone than while we are still here.

It's About How We Finish

In relationships, it's not only about how we start, but also how we finish. Our strength and effectiveness in taking responsibility can be measured by the people who relate to us and trust us. Is there anyone who will still believe in you and adhere to your wisdom?

Let us never refuse the opportunity to step up to the plate. Let us choose to be grateful for the gifts, talents and abilities bestowed upon us and continue to have an attitude of gratitude even in the midst of our storms. Let us allow King David to teach us how to become a true first responder in crisis.

Everyone has a cause. For those of you who take responsibility, much more awaits you. You will never know how exciting life can be unless you take personal responsibility.

Discussion Questions for Chapter 7
"Taking Personal Responsibility"

NAME: _____

DATE: _____

1. What benefits has your personality and
   divine gifts added to your relationships?

   _____

   _____

   _____

   _____

   _____

2. How can you intentionally use your gifts to
   take up the cause of others?

   _____

   _____

   _____

   _____

   _____

3. Are you the solitary one in your family or can you identify the one? Explain your answer.

_____

_____

_____

_____

_____

4. Are there any Goliath-sized challenges in the lives of others that you feel compelled to defeat for them?

_____

_____

_____

_____

_____

— Your Reflections —

CHAPTER 8

Much More Awaits You

But as it is written, Eye hath not seen, nor ear heard, neither have entered into the heart of man, the things which God hath prepared for them that love him.   1 Corinthians 2:9

We must acknowledge that there are serious problems in our world. Many millions of people are suffering from hunger, poverty, lack of medical care, poor educational systems and horrific housing. On top of that, there are floods, fires, earthquakes, hurricanes and wars that take thousands of innocent lives and leave devastation in their wake.

What's more, we still haven't discovered a cure for HIV/AIDS, diabetes or cancer, just to name a few. You would think that these things would sound an alarm and force us to upgrade our lives to position ourselves for a higher purpose.

Experiencing the Devastation of Katrina

In 2005 I experienced one of the most life-changing devastations of my fifty plus years. For the first time in history, a mandatory hurricane evacuation was issued for our New Orleans area, and my wife and I, along with three of our grand-children, were forced to flee to Houston, taking only what we could carry in our hands.

I was under the assumption that we would be away for only a few days, until our area was declared safe to return, but it turned out to be many months before we could even think about going home. As we waited it out, the months quickly turned into a full year, all because of the devastation caused by hurricane Katrina. (By the way, the name *Katrina* means "cleansing.")

As hard as we were hit by the storm and its aftermath and as much as we lost, nothing could replace the wonderful relationships we developed during that crisis. My Katrina experience gave me an entirely new level of compassion. Through Katrina and its aftermath I fostered many new and valuable relationships and friendships. Katrina showed me that a crisis can bring out the best in people who find a cause and take responsibility for helping each other.

Suddenly We Were the Ones in Need

For years our ministry back in New Orleans had reached out to those in need, especially in times of desperation. We had served needy families, the homeless, those suffering from depression and addiction and teenagers who just needed direction in life.

> *My Katrina experience gave me an entirely new level of compassion!*

Katrina now opened our eyes, and we understood that life could change overnight for any of us and without asking our permission. Anyone could be adversely affected, and it was now our turn.

The search for a place to live and the weight and responsibility of headship to provide for my wife and three grandchildren were stressful and began to take their toll on me. We were forced to move from place to place, and our FEMA funding was nearly depleted, and I didn't know where to turn for help.

Needing an Apartment

When it became apparent that we could not go home for a while yet, I began searching for an apartment so that we could stop living from pillar to post and sleeping in our SUV when no hotel rooms were available for us. How we were going to pay for an apartment I wasn't quite sure, but we were desperate.

I found a vacant apartment, and was about to sign a lease for it when a young lady I had never met before came in. When she saw me filling out the application, she said, "Excuse me, sir, could you step outside for a minute?" Once we were outside, she very kindly revealed to me that there were vouchers available through a nearby Presbyterian church and that, through them, I could secure additional assistance for renting any available apartment in Houston.

I went back inside to excuse myself, asking if I could return later to complete the application process. The management of the apartment complex agreed, and off I went, about five miles up the road, to apply for rental assistance. Two days later, it was approved.

"The Other Things You Need"

When I went back to that church to finalize things, they inquired about my wife. She and the kids were visiting a friend. The church staff asked me to go and get her because there was something they wanted to give my wife.

When we returned, they asked questions about our ministry. When we had answered their queries, they responded, "You didn't think that we would give you an apartment without giving you the other things you need?" To our surprise, after years of always giving to others, we were about to be swept off our feet by the compassion and kindness of that church. It finally dawned on us that we were now the ones who were in need and hurting, and it was time to allow others

> When they told us what they intended to do, my wife and I both began weeping uncontrollably at the same time!

to step into their assigned roles and take responsibility to love and serve us.

Food, Clothing and Furniture

In addition to providing housing, the church furnished us with food, clothing and furniture. When they told us what they intended to do, my wife and I both began weeping uncontrollably at the same time. Katrina had caused people to look deep within their hearts and to give more than usual. For us, it ushered in a new experience of people loving and caring for others in a most gracious way.

During those dark days, all across America people were moved with compassion to open their doors and to share their lives with complete strangers who had never crossed their paths before. When there is common pain, there is common gain. Crisis has a way of bringing out the worst and the best in us. To be exposed, exploited and embarrassed was painful, but in the end, it was an invaluable experience because the world benefited, as thousands of people upgraded their compassion.

Much More Awaited Us

Much more awaited us on the other side of this crisis. Governmental change was one of the most important blessings that came out of what thousands of us New Orleanians went through. FEMA and city protocols, procedures and crisis policies were rewritten and upgraded to better serve the needs of suffering people in the future.

I like using this word *upgrade* because through crisis we are forced to update our technology in order to enhance community and governmental relations. Katrina showed us how quickly things can change and why it's crucial to be prepared for healthy relationships. There is much more awaiting those who are prepared for the best of life during the worst of times.

It Makes Sense

It makes sense to concentrate on relationships that really matter to get us to our destiny. Daring to believe and making bold moves will be required. This is an important component of choosing to upgrade and being in the right position for God's best to work in our lives.

With so much going on all around us, relationships activate the ingredients that help us become the people we are meant to be. With today's demands to become fruitful and provide real solutions, we must not delay by playing games with our daily lives.

There is no time to waste. Be encouraged and upgrade in every aspect of life — no matter what it costs or requires of you. Just get it done, and get it done as soon as possible. Make this a priority, and you will bring glory to the Creator. Having a right relationship with God opens the door for a lifetime of meaningful living among your fellowmen.

It Is a Privilege to Be Alive Today

It is a privilege to be alive in this season, when knowledge has increased and the opportunity to learn and advance is within reach for anyone willing to pay the price and make the necessary sacrifices to change. We are blessed to be living in a high-tech, globally-aware, and environmentally green-conscious world. We are benefiting from faster and cleaner transportation, online universities and shopping and, often, the ability to do our life's work from home — if we so choose.

In this age of Facebook, YouTube, MySpace, and Twitter, we have many more ways to communicate with each other, but nothing can replace forming and maintaining good relationships. Technology can enhance our relationships, but it should never replace them.

As the needs of humanity increase, the opportunity to live life to its fullest is challenging. But if we assume responsibility for our cause and decide to live with a greater sense of purpose (and not just for ourselves), we can begin to explore and move to new frontiers and, in the process, upgrade our relationships — beginning with our relationship with God.

"Eye Hath Not Seen"

God's Word says: *"Eye hath not seen, nor ear heard, neither have entered into the heart of man,* the things which God hath prepared for them that love him" (1 Corinthians 2:9). Neither you nor I can imagine how much more awaits us. We can benefit from modern technology and continue to experience the fullness of strong relationships.

I hope that, thus far, this book has been helpful, and I pray that you will use what you have learned as tools for developing healthy long-term relationships.

My Prayer

Let me open my heart to you by offering a prayer to assist you in finding the right relationships and staying on course. Please repeat the prayer after me:

Father, Jehovah, God of all creation and relationships,

I come to You for help, and I repent of trying to do things in my own strength. My greatest desire is to please You and to be all You have created me to be.
I have learned through this book that I must take responsibility for my calling and purpose

in life. I can no longer blame others for my own sin and lack.

I desire to be the solitary one in my family who will obey You all the way. I surrender my life to You, and I acknowledge that the best relationship that I can ever have begins with You. I understand that relationships are doors to help find purpose in life.

Father, You sent Your Son to be the Door to Your Kingdom. On this day, I acknowledge that Christ Jesus, Your only begotten Son, died and rose again so that I could be saved. I acknowledge Jesus as my Lord, and I now commit to being a disciple who grows and honors You with my life. Thank You, Father

I pray that you will use what you have learned as tools for developing healthy long-term relationships!

In Jesus' name I pray.
Amen!

Always remember: *The Foundation for Purpose Is Relationship.*

Discussion Questions for Chapter 8
"Much More Awaits You"

NAME: _____

DATE: _____

1. How have the good relationships in your life caused you to become a better person?

_____

_____

_____

_____

_____

2. How can you create an environment to form better relationships?

_____

_____

_____

_____

_____

3. Can you identify the relationships in your life that open doors to your destiny?

_____

_____

_____

_____

_____

— Your Reflections —

CHAPTER 9

The Interlude

A man that hath friends must shew himself friendly: and there is a friend that sticketh closer than a brother. Proverbs 18:24

There are some things about relationships you will never be able to change, but there are things each of us can do to create an atmosphere for better relationships. No one can serve or love every single person with the same intensity. Even with very best friends, there must be boundaries and limitations that prevent us from overextending ourselves.

The final part of this book will lay a foundation for building strong relationships, or "courting," as I call it. I liken the level of our relationships to the three courts of the ancient Tabernacle. They are: the Outer Court, the Inner Court and the Most

Naked Place. [1] These are your ABCs for relationships, and once you can comprehend what I am about to write, you will develop the patience and understanding needed to attract and retain strong relationships going forward.

Don't Just Rush In

To get to the place of having healthy relationships, you don't just rush in and become completely intimate immediately. If you are doing this, then let me say that your walls are already broken down, and you need to first repair them. Relationships are only useful to you when

> *To get to the place of having healthy relationships, you don't just rush in and become completely intimate immediately!*

---

1. It was called the Most Holy Place or Holy of Holies, but I call it the Naked or Most Naked Place because this stage of relationship requires complete transparency.

you take your time and choose your friends and intimates wisely.

Outer-Court Relationships

The first court, the Outer Court, provides time needed to really get to know someone. Time, in this sense, is not just based on the number of hours, days or years you spend with someone. It is more dependent on the quality of the time and the degree to which you are willing to sacrifice for that person. This is the first step in giving someone your attention.

Many of our friendships are Outer-Court relationships. The Outer Court represents the first area of courting that deals with the lowest level of responsibility. No real "heavy stuff" is needed. This is the stage of getting acquainted, and during this courting period, you may get to know where this person lives, works, plays and worships. You may get to know their friends, family, co-workers and neighbors.

In this stage, you want to be kind, courteous, respectful and slightly inquisitive, just so that you can get answers to some of your preliminary questions. This may be the beginning of a lifelong relationship, or it may just be a passing experience. But you should never truly write someone off when you have just meet them.

This is what I call Level A of courting and communicating. Everyone usually puts his or her best foot forward at this level. However, if you are going to continue on, eventually things will become more challenging. Remember: we are people who love to live in our comfort bubble, so it's hard for us to get over ourselves or come out of ourselves.

This first level is usually not very easy, but get ready because the next court will absolutely burst your bubble. No honeymoon goes on forever. Your feet will soon hit the ground hard, and it may feel as if someone has stolen your shoes.

Inner-Court Relationships

The next level of relationship is what I call the Inner Court or Level B. This is when the relationship becomes a test, and the heart is tried. The true motives for the relationship are revealed, and guess what comes to help facilitate this? Conflict, conflict and more conflict.

As conflict arises, a period of confrontation begins. In Level B, you will get burned. Depending upon your attitude, these conflicts and confrontations can bring with them the fire needed to purify all motives. At this point, most people run back to Court A because they have not yet learned how to handle confrontation well.

Most People Bail Out

This is the point where most people bail out of relationships, refusing to press beyond the conflict and confrontation, allowing their emotions to get the best of them. Most people prefer to spend their time being shallow because they are not secure enough to face confrontation and handle conflict. We are often afraid to lose our identity or discover who we really are and who we are not. We stop thinking about the value that we can give each other, not realizing that the outcome could be a win-win situation. In this way, we miss the victory that comes on the other side of the conflict.

Just imagine what it will be like for the person who endures the fire and rises higher. There is a need for more conflict-resolution skills in relationships. In these final chapters, you will find some thoughts that can help you go beyond the conflicts of this second level of courting.

At times, it may become necessary to move on, once you have attempted to resolve conflicts, and have exhausted every available means, and nothing more can be done. If and when this happens, you should feel free to move on with peace of mind. But, if the due diligence process has not been completed, cutting and running will only reflect your immaturity and lack of skill in relationships.

The Need for Fierce Conversations

We desperately need to have fierce conversations. This is when we get serious about resolving conflicts and making a greater effort to be understood, while respecting the views of others. To illustrate, most of our cities are suffering — politically, socially and economically — because leaders have not committed themselves to studying, developing and maintaining healthy relationships. When we learn how to get beyond disagreements and conflicts without losing the value of friendship, we will transform neighborhoods.

If you don't take time to stop, assess a given situation and make changes in the way you deal with problem relationships, it just might come back to bite you. When you are open to making real improvements, help can be found. We must learn how to honestly face the uncomfortable challenges in relationships. In doing so, we will be more honest and transparent with others.

The joy of enduring the second court, or Level B, brings greater fulfillment in a relationship, and we are then able to enter the C Court.

Our Naked-Place Relationships

I call this third court the Naked Place or the Court of Relationships. When you

Of the due diligence process has not been completed, cutting and running will only reflect your immaturity and lack of skill in relationships!

reach this level, you are now geared up for the rewards of being patient, compassionate and understanding with your family and friends. This comes after the hell and high waters experienced through misunderstandings, hurts and unexpected situations. It is all part of the journey of relating. So don't get discouraged when you are right at the point of breaking into a true C relationship.

As God's Word declares: *"A man that hath friends must shew himself friendly: and there is a friend that sticketh closer than a brother"* (Proverbs 18:24). Transparency brings intimacy, and intimacy will eventually evolve into soul ties.

Is It Worth It?

Now here is the question we must always ask ourselves: "Is this person worth my soul being tied to him (or her)?" The C in the C Court also stands for covenant. It is at this point that we must set (and respect) personal boundaries of how much of ourselves we are willing to give to another. In this court, we decide when and where to make covenant with others.

This type of friendship must be chosen with caution, carefulness, compassion and wisdom. We must not give our soul to just anyone. The other courts provide the process, so when we finally find someone to be in covenant relationship with, we are not needy, but selective.

Love Is Required

All covenant relationships require something you like or love about a person, which has some collaborative benefits. This exceeds feelings, because we choose to like, love and to give to this person. We have to give proper credence to assess the value of the relationship before we make a commitment of any kind.

This is something real for us, now that we know that relationships can propel us deeper into our purpose. The heart of this C Court is the willingness to serve others with the gifts with which we've been blessed. As a result, we become stronger and better. Confidence, assurance, faith, hope and love are all graceful platforms that will enrich us as well as others. Rejoice in your new wave of healthy friendships!

Remembering the three courts — A or Outer Court, B or Inner Court and C or the Naked Place — will help you obtain good relationships.

Building relationships is a process that requires a lot of effort!

Advancing These Three Courts

In the remaining chapters, we will take a look at what I consider to be the most valuable and practical ways to purposefully advance through these three courts. Building relationships is a process that requires a lot of effort. We will need skills and the ability to move forward cautiously so that we don't destroy those who are sent to help us.

As the Scriptures teach:

He that covereth a transgression seeketh love; but he that repeateth a matter separateth very friends.   Proverbs 17:9

Faithful are the wounds of a friend; but the kisses of an enemy are deceitful.   Proverbs 27:6

Iron sharpeneth iron; so a man sharpeneth the countenance of his friend.   Proverbs 27:17

A friend loveth at all times, and a brother is born for adversity.   Proverbs 17:17

Never forget: *The Foundation of Purpose Is Relationship.*

Discussion Questions for Chapter 9
"The Interlude"

NAME: _____

DATE: _____

1. Are most of your relationships Outer-Court experiences or Inner-Court experiences? Explain.

_____

_____

_____

_____

_____

2. Have your relationships been dissolved or sustained at the Outer-Court level?

_____

_____

_____

_____

_____

3. What are some effective ways to handle the conflicts and confrontations that arise at the Inner-Court level?

_____

_____

_____

_____

_____

4. Can you describe one relationship in your life that successfully transitioned from the Outer Court to the Naked Place?

_____

_____

_____

_____

_____

— Your Reflections —

CHAPTER 10

Humility

Yea, all of you be subject one to another, and be clothed with humility: for God resisteth the proud, and giveth grace to the humble.

1 Peter 5:5

The next four chapters will provide what you need to develop quality relationships. Your journey will be useless if you have read and accepted the previous nine chapters and then you strike out at this point. As you step up to the batter's box, the plays we have shared have given you practice in building better relationships. Now here is what is needed for a successful completion of your journey.

The first thing is humility. What is humility? It is "the quality of being humble." You will find security in your relationships when the spirit of humility is present and you choose to prefer others. You do not have to love others more than you love yourself to prefer them.

What Humility Is Not

Humbling ourselves and walking in humility does not mean that we are afraid to be ourselves. Being humble does not mean that we are intimidated by the successes, talents and resources of others. There is no need to allow others to walk all over you. A humble person can still speak up when necessary.

Humility does just the opposite. When we are secure, we can bring what is needed to be a part of the team. Humility clears the way for us to continue relating to others. It creates a less defensive atmosphere, which allows us to bring our best to the table and then also to bring out the best in others.

Humility says to others, "You are valuable, and I respect the reason we are together." It allows us to mine for the gold in others. Humility says, "I know who I am, but I see something in you that I need." It disarms pride and the desire to show off. It makes us uncomfortable with boasting.

Humility reveals who we are, not what we do to prove ourselves. It says, "I accept you. No facade is needed. You don't need to perform in order to be accepted." Humility will relax you.

Humility Goes Further

Humility goes even further and says, "I can see beyond your shortcomings, mistakes and sins and still choose to serve you." This is what makes humility so powerful. It keeps the person who is humble aware that no one is perfect, including him- or herself. It helps us to remember that we wouldn't have made it through our own personal crises without the mercy of others.

> *Humbling ourselves and walking in humility does not mean that we are afraid to be ourselves!*

Humility will always help us hit it off well with others. It's natural to have a strong defensive wall to prevent us from hurt. However, I believe that we all need to grow out of this, so that we do not spend most of our time protecting ourselves. The hallmark of our growth is to feel good about who we are and be humble in the presence of others.

Humility gives honest people the opportunity to share their talents, skills and abilities. False humility does just the opposite. It is not real humility when we walk away withholding what we have to offer. False humility robs the relationship of its value. This type of behavior usually stems from a fear of rejection and/or a lack of courage.

When we are truly humble, we are not afraid to take responsibility for what we have to say. And when we are wrong, we can accept correction. True humility doesn't try to prove what is right; it allows one's character to reveal what is real.

Walking in False Humility

When we hold things back and miss opportunities to be heard, we are walking in false humility (and sometimes stupidity). True humility will help us navigate through the fog and get to the real issues in our relationships.

However, in all of this, we must have a spirit of true humility. Pride looks out for itself, while humility looks out for others. The bottom line is this: we cannot afford to keep missing opportunities for any reason. We must seize the moment, for there is no guarantee that such an opportunity will come along again. If we continue to hold back and prevent our gifts and talents from blessing others, soon that window or door will shut, and our blessings be given to someone else.

If you are talented, bright and capable of doing more with your life, but you can't figure out what's holding you back, you are probably walking in false humility. Your best friends probably don't know who you really are, because you have been holding back in those relationships. This is not only their loss, but it also causes fear and rejection to dominate the relationship and hinders you from giving your best.

The opposite of fear and rejection is love and acceptance, which will provide the context to walk in true humility with value. In the end, humility will honor you, as you honor others, and allow you to exceed your greatest expectations. Humility in relationships will allow you to be great without the need to crush others. So, whatever you do, don't strike out at humility.

Discussion Questions for Chapter 10 "Humility"

NAME: _____

DATE: _____

1. What is humility? Explain your answer.

_____

_____

_____

_____

_____

2. What type of atmosphere does humility create?

_____

_____

_____

_____

_____

3. What is one of the things that humility says?
   And how does that statement relate to you?

   _____

   _____

   _____

   _____

   _____

4. What does false humility say? Explain your
   answer (see pages 152-153).

   _____

   _____

   _____

   _____

   _____

5. True humility allows you to be great without
   crushing others. Do you consider yourself to
   be humble?

   _____

   _____

   _____

   _____

6. How could you show more humility toward
   others?

   _____
   _____
   _____
   _____
   _____

— Your Reflections —

CHAPTER 11

Respect

Let nothing be done through strife or vainglory; but in lowliness of mind let each esteem other better than themselves. Look not every man on his own things, but every man also on the things of others. Philippians 2:3-4

The next important element is respect. What is respect? "Having deferential regard for, to esteem, to express consideration." In the early 1970s, Aretha Franklin sang, "All I'm asking for is a little respect. R-E-S-P-E-C-T! Find out what it means to me!" Oddly enough, her cry reflects one of the most important needs in all human relationships. If you strike out at this, you may be better off being alone, for the pivotal factor in how well a relationship develops is mutual respect.

More Than Just a Little

We need more than just a little bit of respect for one another; we need a lot. Respect is the fuel that keeps the fire burning in relationships.

> *Respect is the fuel that keeps the fire burning in relationships!*

Respect is undermined when we are critical, judgmental, biased, prejudiced, unforgiving, impatient, angry, fearful, inconsiderate or controlling. Such issues make life challenging and the building of healthy relationships difficult. They also make life stressful. Usually people who force others to respect them are the ones who fall short in respecting others.

What we have come to call the Golden Rule says, "Do unto others as you would have them do unto you. " It can be helpful to remind ourselves that whatever we sow, we shall also reap (see Galatians 6:7). You may have heard the popular saying: Hurting people will hurt other people?

Usually the root cause is that somewhere along the line respect was not given, and rejection took root or continued to grow.

Respect is vital if you are to touch a person's heart. It has the power to turn a relationship around. Your respect will increase the quality of trust and begin to restore what was lacking in earlier relationships.

Even When They Don't Deserve it

It is important to give respect to others, even when they don't deserve it. This is called common courtesy. Even if someone doesn't want your respect, it is wise to give it to everyone, because we are all created by God and in His image. Respect other people, even when you don't share their beliefs. Respect people of different races and cultures and of differing opinions.

Even if you know negative things about a person, respect them anyway. Respect means giving consideration, and being considerate can go a long way toward changing someone's heart. Respect the poor, the handicapped, the mentally ill and people who are different from you. Be kind to those who are sick and in the hospital, the elderly and those who are in prison. Prisoners may need your respect more than anyone else. Everyone needs to know that they are still human and that God sent His Son to die for them. Showing respect has a way of touching someone's heart. It opens the door for new and better things.

Even When They Don't Respect Themselves

Give others respect, even if they don't respect themselves. When you do this, God will reward you. Everyone craves respect, and those who master giving it will have many friends. When our lives come to an end, the only thing that will matter is whether our relationships have influenced others and enhanced their lives. Respect can go a long way to make this happen and so can loving someone unconditionally.

We don't have to be pleased with someone's behavior or attitude to show them that we love them. On our side of the relationship, let us not fail in the area of respect.

The way someone treats us when conflicts emerge may be the fruit of deeper problems.

We degrade ourselves when we disrespect the people who love us most. There will be tension when our children, friends, parents, spouses and co-workers seek to serve their own desires. However, don't allow this to cause you to lose respect for them.

There is an old saying: "Those convinced against their will are of the same opinion still." Respect allows people the space to do stupid things, even when it may harm them or others. Still, show them respect.

You may expect others to respect you, because you respect others, but you must remember that no one is required to respect you. We should ask ourselves this: "Do we respect others and encourage them to live their best life? Or are we so hard on others that nobody wants to be close to us?"

The great master of relationships is Jesus. He skillfully managed to give respect to everyone. Consequently ordinary and sinful people spent more time with Him than with the religious leaders of their day. If Jesus walked down our streets today, He would be surrounded by people who are hurting, downtrodden and outcast, because even if they don't deserve it, He would give them what they need: RESPECT!

If we strike out with respect, this, no doubt, indicates that we have also struck out with humility. That's two strikes.

Discussion Questions for Chapter 11
"Respect"

NAME: _____

DATE: _____

1. How can showing respect to others enhance your relationships with them? Explain your answer.

   _____

   _____

   _____

   _____

   _____

2. Do you express unconditional respect for others — even if you don't agree with their behavior? Explain your answer.

   _____

   _____

   _____

   _____

   _____

3. How has being respected positively impacted your personal life?

_____

_____

_____

_____

_____

— Your Reflections —

CHAPTER 12

Yielding

To every thing there is a season, and a time to every purpose under the heaven.

Ecclesiastes 3:1

After the chapters on humility and respect, we are all set for the final ingredient — yielding. If we are truthful, we can look back and see that some relationships were just practice for others. Although no one wants to be thought of as the person whom others practice on or the person who practices on others, it's still true. The experience prepares you to develop relationships for the future. Times and seasons will come and go, but what we do with each season makes all the difference in developing enjoyable and productive relationships.

The simple principle we will discuss in this chapter makes win-win relationships possible, and that principles is yielding in our season and knowing when it's time to let go.

What Do We Mean by Yielding?

To yield is "to give up possession on claim or demand, to surrender, to give up an inclination, temptation or habit." Humility and respect are both used in serving, but they are different as they relate to the heart. Humility serves by preferring others, while respect serves in deferring to others. The final ingredient is simple yet profound: Just yield!

You can walk in humility and truly respect others, but the purpose of each season will be different. We can't change seasons, but the season will change us. The essential challenge is found in that old serenity prayer attributed to the American theologian Reinhold Niebuhr (1892–1971):

God grant me the serenity to accept the things
I cannot change,
The courage to change the things I can,
And the wisdom to know the difference.

This prayer asks for the wisdom to know when to hold on and when to let go, and to know the difference. This is what seasons are like in relationships. We will strike out if we do not yield appropriately to the people in our lives in a particular season. And if you strike out here, then your hope and faith are small.

We Have to Believe in Others

We have to believe in others in order to yield to them. So keep in mind that there is good inside of everyone. Yielding, however, begins with listening and attempting to be agreeable. This is the test: Can we listen to others, receive their thoughts and then adjust and change our ways as needed? Or are we so stubborn that we refuse to change?

Do we attack the person who is trying to help us, in order to defend ourselves? Do we

God grant me the serenity to accept the things I cannot change!

feel we are always right? Or can we admit when we are wrong? Is saying, "I'm sorry," too hard for us to do? Are we willing to accept things even when we are sure we are right? The answers to all these questions will tell us if we are ready to have better relationships or not.

To yield is to be the first to ask for forgiveness when needed. If a person has shown no humility and no respect and is not willing to yield, they have struck out and will not have laid the groundwork needed for successfully relating to others. The reality of life is this: after these three strikes, you're out.

Relationships Are Determined by the Seasons

Relationships are determined by the seasons, but purpose is established by relationship. There will be times when we need advice, so before you strike out, seek wise counsel. This may protect your destiny and release the power of relationship for you. Even the worst relationships can become the best for you — if you can admit that you need help.

Yielding

I hope you will use this book to help you discover your destiny. If you've been alone because you struck out once or more than once, and you're tired of trying, I have this advice for you: your life does not have to end negatively. You may need to read this book a few times before you can put its principles into practice. But you were created for a purpose, and it's time to let your relationships lead you to it.

Destiny Awaits

Remember that God has your best interests at heart. Destiny awaits those who have faith, so work on being better, and find ways to live a creative and full life. My prayer is that this book will increase the value you place on relating well with others and help to identify and bring clarity to your relationships.

Most of all, I hope that you can see that just as you are unique and worthy of respect, others are too. So treat everyone with honesty and sincerity. Be who you are, without compromising your integrity. But, at the same time, allow others to also be who they really are. Then, at the end of the day, only carry your own burdens.

Your Best Days Are Here

Your best days are not just around the corner; they are here. So enjoy engaging with others, for that is God's gift to you.

Other people are human, just like you. Decide to be in fellowship with others without any strings attached. Just do it. You will find that having fun is not a sin. Strong relationships will lead you to your destiny. Always remember: *The Foundation for Purpose Is Relationship.*

But the book has not concluded. You must read the final chapter to brace yourself for this journey to better relationships. If you are to finish strong, you have to plan to finish strong. In order to do this, give yourself a few moments to read the final chapter: "When the Honeymoon Is Over."

Discussion Questions for Chapter 12
"Yielding"

NAME: _____

DATE: _____

1. Do you actively listen to others with the intent to be agreeable? Explain your answer.

_____

_____

_____

_____

_____

2. Have you learned how to yield during times of disagreement?

_____

_____

_____

_____

_____

3. Do you see the value of yielding in relationships?

_____

_____

_____

_____

_____

— Your Reflections —

CHAPTER 13

When the Honeymoon Is Over

But the LORD said unto Samuel, Look not on his countenance, or on the height of his stature; because I have refused him: for the LORD seeth not as man seeth; for man looketh on the outward appearance, but the LORD looketh on the heart.

1 Samuel 16:7

Honeymoon can be defined as: "1. A vacation or trip taken by a newly-married couple, 2. the month or so following a marriage, 3. any period of blissful harmony, 4. any new relationship characterized by an initial period of harmony and goodwill. (The honeymoon between Congress and the new President was over.)" [1]

_____

1. American Dictionary of the English Language

Every Relationship Will Go through Seasons

In concluding this book, I must remind you of the reality that every relationship will go through seasons. The most startling time may be when the honeymoon is over. Some people are great and awesome at task management. However, when it comes to having to deal with relationships, the light goes off and withdrawal begins because they prefer not to get too close to anyone. Some people are great at details and enjoy taking charge and making things happen, but people who handle details well may sometimes get frustrated with those who are visionaries and dreamers.

> *Sooner or later, all honeymooners have to deal with their differences!*

Visionaries are always thinking about the next project or new risk they are ready to undertake, while the manager type is saying, "Wait! We haven't finished what we have already started!"

Sooner or later, all honeymooners have to deal with their differences. Even though each is needed in the relationship, the reality of the problems that surface threaten to bring the honeymoon to an abrupt end.

Let Us Go Deeper

Let us go deeper. There are those who insist on living by their principles, but they fail to realize that principles without compassion are useless and senseless. There are those who believe that doing what is right, for them, matters more than maintaining proper relationships. Some put their laws, principles and external values above the human heart, totally missing what God said to the prophet Samuel about Saul:

> *Look not on his countenance, or on the height of his stature; because I have refused him: for the Lord seeth not as man seeth; for man looketh on the outward appearance, but the Lord looketh on the heart.* 1 Samuel 16:7

It is possible to live a honeymoon life-style, basing everything on outward appearances, while at the same time consuming material things at the expense of genuine relationships. Life is more than things, and it takes time to really get to know someone. Because God looks at the heart, we need to do likewise. We need to see others from His perspective. Just because things seem to be going well on the outside does not mean that the person is truly developing on the inside.

What I'm saying here is that a relationship that can be vitally important to us must get beyond the honeymoon stage. We all enter into relationships with our "stuff" and our issues that are not immediately apparent. The truth about life is that human relationships are complex, different and unique, but they all lead to one same reality. That reality is that no matter where we begin with someone, we cannot live and fulfill our destiny as honeymooners.

Celebratory Seasons Always End

The celebratory season will one day come to a crashing halt, and the joy that we once had will be challenged with the call to something that, by any and all means, we were intending to avoid. But real relationships endure, even when things

get tough. Just as any marriage cannot survive on honeymoon expectations, our relationships that will be used to contribute to our purpose cannot exist always on vacation mode.

You cannot expect valuable relationships to survive or thrive just on a honeymoon experience. The sooner the relationship awakens from the honeymoon, the better it will be for its future. Those who attempt to enjoy and continue their marriage with a honeymoon mind-set will not be developed and mature enough to fulfill their God-given potential, simply because the best in any relationship is not brought out by a vacation alone.

A vacation, like a honeymoon, serves as a time of rest, relaxation and refreshment. However the truth is that when you come out of that getaway, the thing you desired to avoid is what you must now face, if you are to succeed. This will require what is commonly called "consistent hard work."

Do the Hard Work

In concluding this book, my desire is to encourage you to put some hard effort into yourself and others. The best of relationships will take a lot of love, forgiveness, honesty and hard work on the areas where improvement is needed.

The fact that the honeymoon is over simply means that it is time to stop trying to win by placing your best foot forward. Now it is time to move by working to placing your whole life, mind and heart into the relationship. Therefore, as you give your best to others, others will be drawn to give their best to you.

Learning to Work Smart

It has been said that we should not always work hard, but rather work smart. This is usually true when referring to an occupation, a career improvement or earning more money. However, this principle may not work when it comes to relationships, because people are more than a statistic, job or paycheck. To have a relationship with others, it is not always what you can get out of them. In some cases, it will be what you can give that will cause you to be a better person. To achieve significance is to have influence, weight and substance that impacts others through relationship.

Our Greatest Rewards

Some of the greatest rewards come when we help others who cannot pay us in return. This is why relationships will sometimes require hard work to get to the breaking point, where change really does happen, because someone hung in there consistently enough to make it happen.

A relationship that can be vitally important to us must get beyond the honeymoon stage!

The homeless, poor, handicapped, elderly, mentally challenged, war victims, divorcees and countless more unnamed all need relationships, for God made us social beings that all have a deep desire to be accepted and loved. How can we ever make our world better, if we never get beyond our selfish desire to remain on a honeymoon?

This is why I believe that every potentially good relationship has the ability to prepare us to experience things we cannot imagine on our own. This process of evolving from the honeymoon to real life will propel us to come out of ourselves and begin to participate in our true calling in life. This may not be success as we have known it, but it surely will be significance.

In closing, may grace and peace be multiplied to you, for you will need it. Have fun while you learn, and never stop learning. And always remember: *The Foundation for Purpose Is Relationship.*

Discussion Questions for Chapter 13
"When the Honeymoon Is Over"

NAME: _____

DATE: _____

1. Are you willing to go beyond the honey-moon phase to form genuine relationships?

   _____
   _____
   _____
   _____
   _____

2. Do you allow your principles and external values to prohibit the formation of valuable relationships? Explain your answer.

   _____
   _____
   _____
   _____
   _____

3. Have you ever aborted relationships because of your lack of tools to progress beyond the honeymoon phase? Discuss this.

_____

_____

_____

_____

_____

4. Are there any relationships that you need to take responsibility to restore and usher beyond the Outer-Court experience? Explain your answer.

_____

_____

_____

_____

_____

— Your Reflections —

Author Contact Page

If this book has been a blessing to you, I would love to hear from you. You may contact me in any of the following ways:

Apostle Reginald H. Wilson, Sr.

Phone: (504) 270-4928

www.reggiewilsonministries.com
www.facebook.com/Globalh?fref=ts

Email: rwcontact@reggiewilsonministries.com

www.ingramcontent.com/pod-product-compliance
Lightning Source LLC
LaVergne TN
LVHW051233080426
835513LV00016B/1568